This may be a little [...]
Heartfelt,
DAI

"I HEART

'A wonderful lit
happini

SARA WHEELER, BUSINESS CONSULTANT

First published in United Kingdom by Ingram Spark 2017

First Edition

ISBN 978-0-9956272-2-2

A Little Book of Happiness

FOR

FROM

Filled with Joy

'Explore, Dream, Discover'
MARK TWAIN

FOREWORD
BY ELIZA WRENNE
MUSICIAN & RUNNER

' Yes! I was so excited when I heard Kim & Jake were putting together a little book. Her expert thoughts, spoken through her Hound of Happiness are made of pearls and I want to collect them all, for myself and my daughter.

If you are on a journey to discovering your authentic self or just looking for a ray of happiness, these tips will only delight and help you as a source of weekly inspiration.

So put your phone down and tune into your own inner self with these practical, positive tips, on your own or with your family. Dip into the Hound of Happiness for a month and I can guarantee you will all be better for it!'

Thank you for buying my little Book, packed full of tips to help you feel good. My name is Jake, the Hound of Happiness and I live with my owner, Kim. I've had three homes and sometimes get a little bit anxious, doubt myself and find it hard to trust. Other times I can get really excited, play, and run for miles. It really depends on the day.

My owner Kim helps me to feel good by giving me clear boundaries and routines, as well as reassuring me and having lots of fun. I've learned to trust and enjoy life again, eating great food, having good sleep and starting to believe in myself.

We wanted to write this book to help bring you simple tips for happiness. I often see people getting worried and stuck, not feeling well or having any fun. So I hope that this little book helps you to feel good and have some fun in every week. You can work through the book, week by week or just dip in and out, choosing the tip that feels right for the moment.

Whatever, we hope it brings you helpful tips to do and feel good. Do let us know how you get on and share your photos with #houndofhappiness,

Big support, wags and happiness from us both, Jake and

8

'It is never too late to be what you may have been'

GEORGE ELIOT

NO. 1

Pause for a moment,
Think of all the good in your life right now,
Write everything down,
Enjoy and celebrate how they make you feel.

Stretch the tight muscles in your body,
Allow your body to relax in the stretch,
Give yourself five minutes daily,
Breathe deeply and feel good.

Each day, stand tall,
Imagine your back lengthening,
From the tip of your head to your toes,
Strengthen your posture.

NO. 4

Move your body today,
Walk, run, dance, cycle, swim,
Feel your heart beating,
Boost your energy and mood.

No. 5

Be beautifully you,
Expressive, funny, creative, strong,
Intelligent, wise, wonderful, calm,
Whatever is you, be your best.

Have good thoughts,
Move towards what you would like to think,
Notice and change thoughts you don't want,
Be positive and patient with yourself.

NO. 7

Sadness is okay,
It's part of life,
Look after you when you feel sad,
Self-care is good.

No. 8

Grow your self belief,
With a pinch of courage,
And a dash of patience,
Allow yourself to believe.

Fear is good,
Because something matters.
Embrace your fears,
And keep moving forwards.

NO. 10

Value yourself,
What makes you, you?
Realise the good in you,
Grow this.

No. 11

Make a decision,
Let go of procrastination,
Pause for a moment,
Allow your life to flow.

NO. 12

Drink plenty of water,
Clear the toxins,
Brighten your eyes and skin,
Boost your well-being.

No. 13

Eat lots of fresh, good foods,
Keep a good variety,
Plan your meals,
Slow down and enjoy.

No. 14

Make each day good,
Choose how you spend your time,
Notice and change habits that waste time,
Focus on creating what you want.

NO. 15

Get creative in the kitchen,
Try a new recipe,
Have fun preparing,
Celebrate your meal with friends.

NO. 16

Go to bed a little earlier,
Switch off your devices,
Drink sleepy tea, pause,
Be peaceful and rest deeply.

No. 17

Observe excellence in others,
Let go of comparison,
Notice what you like,
Go make it happen for you.

No. 18

Spend a time alone,
Be peaceful and quiet,
Tune into your inner wisdom,
Notice how you are.

NO. 19

Learn to know what you like,
And what you do not like,
Let go of what you do not,
Make time for what you do like.

NO. 20

Spend time with good people,
Nurture these relationships,
Add value to your life,
Enhance the lives around you.

NO. 21

Create your happy family,
Give them your time,
Give support when it matters,
Grow memories of value.

Expand your life,
Through experiences that excite you,
And life events which challenge you,
Always be open to growth.

NO. 23

Take your dreams of travel,
And plan your adventure,
Make it happen,
Commit, begin and pack.

NO. 24

Nurture your wealth,
Let go of fear,
Give with gratitude,
Grow an abundant mindset.

No. 25

Create a few little savings,
For a sunshine day of happiness,
Or an unexpected challenge,
Respect and enjoy your money.

No. 26

Make sure you grow,
Your dreams and courage,
Knowledge and experiences,
Beautifully you.

NO. 27

Learn a new skill,
Challenge your brain,
Do not fear being a beginner,
Expand your opportunities.

No. 28

Clear the clutter,
From your home,
And your mind,
Create spaces.

NO. 29

Freshen up your image,
Make it current,
Clothes, style,
Feel alive and energised.

Be compassionate,
To yourself,
And to those around you,
We are all doing the best we can.

NO. 31

Make time for play,
Childlike laughter,
Smiles and relaxation,
Daily, simple fun.

No. 32

Find your passions,
What sparks excitement?
Create space in your life,
For joy to flow regularly.

NO. 33

Be clear on your priorities,
What is important to you right now?
Focus, be committed.
Make time for these now.

No. 34

Awaken your dream,
Create a plan of action,
Remove limits and excuses,
Be accountable.

No. 35

Create your project happiness,
Fill it with daily, tiny good things,
Change your not so good habits,
Build a Happy You.

NO. 36

Give hugs,
To yourself,
And those around you,
It will make you feel good.

No. 37

Take time away,
Change your routine,
Do something different,
Notice what feels good.

NO. 38

Be honest and true,
With yourself,
And those around you,
Self-respect and respect.

NO. 39

Take a deep breath, daily,
Allow your body to pause,
Tune in with how you feel,
Adapt to improve wellness.

Become strong in your body,
Balanced in your muscles,
Fit and fast in your limbs,
See what is possible.

NO. 41

Do something different,
Challenge what is comfortable,
Notice what is possible,
Adapt new things into your life.

NO. 42

Be mindful of your stories,
Let go of past habits and limits,
Share what you want to create,
Act until you believe.

NO. 43

Do not fear the past or future, be present,
Let go of what you cannot control,
Life ebbs and flows, highs and lows,
Learn to enjoy the ride.

NO. 44

Keep it simple,
Think of what could you stop doing?
And what could you start doing?
Simple changes right now.

NO. 45

Give acts of kindness,
To someone who adds value to your life,
And just randomly to help others,
Kindness will come back to you.

NO. 46

Start each day with a positive intention,
Be clear on what you will do,
Be proud of what you did, adapt what you
did not,
Finish with helpful reflections.

No. 47

Find your loves in life,
Learn to love the moment,
Embrace it,
Trust and nurture.

No. 48

Learn to love yourself,
Be vulnerable to love another,
Without losing yourself,
Grow your best together.

NO. 49

Trust in good things,
Let go of fears and doubts,
Self-sabotage and worries,
Welcome hope.

No. 50

Have a little patience,
Sometimes the unknown is where you have to be,
Hold your vision of good,
Be brave, something is possible.

NO. 51

If you ever doubt yourself,
Just pause, look after you,
Take a deep breath,
Keep going, you can do this.

NO. 52

Remember to celebrate,
The moments, in the moment,
Happiness for yourself and others,
Pure contentment and joy.

THE END...

or just your beginning!

'Take a deep breath, follow your heart, make a wish . . .'

STEPHEN BENNETT

Notes *for* YOUR OWN

FEEL GOOD TIPS

HABITS & THOUGHTS

TO CHANGE *this year*

DREAMS & ACTIONS

TO DO *this year*

ABOUT
JAKE & KIM

Jake is a white staffy mixed breed, born some time in 2014 we think. If you met him, he will always great you with a big wag and a smile. He's full of character, a quick learner, loves any kind of ball and big walks. At night he requests a belly rub, before snoring loudly!

His owner, Kim Ingleby is a triple award winning international mind body coach and founder of Energised Performance. She works with Team GB, CEOs, Strictly Come Dancing & Body Confidence. Kim loves adventures, trekking across the Andes on horseback, running in Transylvania and helping Street Child in Sierra Leone. In 2013 she caught weils disease swimming in open water, with secondary encephalitis and is learning to heal her brain and neurology. She has raised over £80,000 for charity and done a TEDx Talk. She loves to run, cook, photograph and wander her super hound Jake. She was born in Scotland, with family in NYC and Jerusalem, while they currently live in Bristol, UK.

WE LOVE YOU
TO GET
INVOLVED...

@KIMINGLEBY
#HOUNDOFHAPPINESS

@KIMINGLEBY
@THEHOUNDOFHAPPINESS
#HOUNDOFHAPPINESS

@KIMINGLEBY
#HOUNDOFHAPPINESS

Visit **WWW.KIMINGLEBY.CO.UK** and sign up to our monthly newsletter, packed full of tips to feel good, competitions & much more.

Email us with your stories: **KIM@KIMINGLEBY.CO.UK** and you could be featured in our monthly newsletter.

Do tag and share your photos with your **#HOUNDOFHAPPINESS** to help spread the feel good message and you never know, you may be picked at random for a 'spot' human or hound prize randomly throughout the year…!

Kim's philosophy has always been to give something back to charity, and has so far raised over £80,000 for charity so far. Each month Kim will donate a little amount from the books she has sold to little Hound and Human Charities and will share in the newsletter every month.

For Mind & Body coaching and support visit Kim's company and find out more:

WWW.ENERGISEDPERFORMANCE.COM

 @ENERGISEDCOACH
#UNLOCKYOURPOTENTIAL
#GAINTHEEDGE

 ENERGISED PERFORMANCE
MENTAL STRENGTH COACHING

For more tips you can watch Kim's TEDx Talk:
HTTPS://YOUTU.BE/E2P8GKJU8HW

THANK YOUS

Wow! I can't believe 'we' did it and this book has come together. I know it's a little book, but I hope it makes a really big difference to everyone who buys it, bringing joy, happiness and courage to feel good in life.

Thank you firstly to Christianne Wolff for coaching, supporting and believing in me to bring this together, you are a star!

For Che Dyer, illustrator and yoga teacher who created the wonderful #houndofhappiness mascot for your life. He believes in you, like we do!

To the amazing graphic designer Lou Banks, who is quite simply brilliant, quite simply brilliant, bringing together my notes, rambles and ideas together into the book you hold in your hands.

To Sara Wheeler who has coached me for years, challenged me massively to improve and proof read this book, thank you.

To all my great clients, all over the World, who have inspired and encouraged me to start writing books, I hope you love this one. There will be more to come, I promise!

To John Wood, for the great photos that capture the wonderful relationship and trust Jake and I have. Thank you for supporting and believing in us and this feel good book.

To the charities who support and help so many hounds and humans, you are amazing, thank you.

To my Hound of Happiness, Jake, thank you for coming into our lives. I hope this book brings you many tennis balls, growing confidence and much love. You have taught me so much, become my best friend and allowed me to and allowed me to trust myself again whilst I continue to heal, thank you. Big pats and wanders always.

There are many more awesome people in my life, you don't even realise how amazing you are, so thank you!

Finally, Thank YOU all for buying this little book of happiness, I hope it helps you (& your hounds!) feel good.

Big love, wags and thanks,

'Live in the Sunshine,
Swim in the Sea,
Drink the Wild Air'

RALPH WALDO
EMERSON

'I highly recommend this lovely little book of wisdom. Allow yourself to be guided by Kim through her Hound of Happiness, and you will surpass your expectations.'
KER TYLER, CEO FIT FOR LEADERSHIP

'A beautiful collection of simple ways to feel good every week. Kim and Jake's tips are bite sized brilliance'
JEN ISAACS, TEAM GB ATHLETE
TRIATHLON AND COMRADES FINISHER

Lightning Source UK Ltd.
Milton Keynes UK
UKOW07f0653070317
296063UK00010B/21/P